Echoes of
CREATION

JEANNE PRINTUP-WESTA

WESTBOW·
PRESS
A DIVISION OF THOMAS NELSON
& ZONDERVAN

Scriptures taken from the Holy Bible, New International Version®, NIV®. Copyright © 1973, 1978, 1984, 2011 by Biblica, Inc.™ Used by permission of Zondervan. All rights reserved worldwide. www.zondervan.com The "NIV" and "New International Version" are trademarks registered in the United States Patent and Trademark Office by Biblica, Inc.™ All rights reserved.

Scripture quotations are from The Holy Bible, English Standard Version® (ESV®), copyright © 2001 by Crossway, a publishing ministry of Good News Publishers. Used by permission. All rights reserved.

WestBow Press books may be ordered through booksellers or by contacting:

WestBow Press
A Division of Thomas Nelson & Zondervan
1663 Liberty Drive
Bloomington, IN 47403
www.westbowpress.com
1 (866) 928-1240

Because of the dynamic nature of the Internet, any web addresses or links contained in this book may have changed since publication and may no longer be valid. The views expressed in this work are solely those of the author and do not necessarily reflect the views of the publisher, and the publisher hereby disclaims any responsibility for them.

Any people depicted in stock imagery provided by Thinkstock are models, and such images are being used for illustrative purposes only. Certain stock imagery © Thinkstock.

ISBN: 978-1-4908-3196-1 (sc)
ISBN: 978-1-4908-3197-8 (e)

Library of Congress Control Number: 2014905767

Printed in the United States of America.

WestBow Press rev. date: 05/21/2014

Contents

Dedication vii

Preface.. ix

Hidden Treasure...1

No Trespassing...2

Take Flight 3

Bugs! 5

Authenticity...6

Release 7

Hope 8

Perspective 9

Protection 10

Transformation 12

Be Still 13

Light..15

Clouds 16

Fences...17

Weathered by Life 19

Unity in the Body...20

Accountability..21

Mushrooms 23

Wounded 24

Effective Image 25

Ripple Effect 26

Open Palms..27

Seasons of Grace..28

Under Attack 30

Oasis...31

Beware! 32

Comfortable 34

Abundant Life 35

Obstacles 36

Passion..38

Abiding...40

Scripture Index...41

Dedication

First and foremost, I dedicate *Echoes of Creation* to my Lord and Savior, Jesus Christ, for it is my personal relationship with Him that made this God-sized dream possible. "'For I know the plans I have for you,' declares the LORD, 'plans to prosper you and not to harm you, plans to give you hope and a future.'" (Jeremiah 29:11)

For my mother, who gave me my first ever journal, inscribed with the words, "Your thoughts are a treasure from God"; little did she know then the dream she would inspire me to accomplish with God's help.

I would also like to recognize my sons, Jason, Jacob, and Timothy, as well as their families, for contributing to the outdoor experiences through which God provided some of the devotional ideas. In addition, I thank Creation Images Photography owners, Jake and Katie Printup, whose God-given talent provided two of the photos among these pages.

To Kem Stickl, Mary Ann Foegen, and JoGee Monroe...my dear friends, mentors, and fellow sisters-in-Christ: thank you for providing godly wisdom, direction, and encouragement that continue to help me grow as a woman of God.

And to my husband, Jon Robert Westa, whose encouragement, love, and support were crucial in bringing this dream to reality. Thank you for believing in me. You are an instrument in God's mighty hands and for that I am truly grateful.

Preface

Words have been an important part of my life from a young age. Playing Scrabble with my siblings and parents, reading (and being read to), competing in spelling bees, and keeping a diary were frequent occurrences in my childhood. When I became a mother of three sons, these were activities that continued into their childhood as well. As an adult, I pursued a degree in Speech-Language Pathology in the hope that my love of words and language, in spoken and written forms, could make a difference for others. As a believer and follower of Jesus, I wanted to use this gift of words he blessed me with to bless others. I eagerly awaited the day when He would lead me to do so.

In April of 2010, the church I belonged to implemented a program entitled "Ready, Set, Go!" to assist members in identifying and connecting their strengths, passions, gifts, and values as a method for getting them involved in service. One of the tasks was to determine a dream you could not accomplish without God's help. After considerable time prayerfully reflecting on past experiences, passions, and strengths, I realized that now was the time to put my love of words to use for God's glory, honor, and praise.

While spending time outdoors gardening, hiking, camping, and other such activities, I had gained insights regarding God's character, His ways, and the truths of His word on occasion. When I contemplated the subject matter of the book He placed on my heart, I sensed God directing me in writing a devotional that made connections between these concepts and creation itself, since creation is a revelation of who God is. Thus began my three year journey of compiling such insights into this book.

Many of the ideas were obtained in the Western New York area, including Niagara Falls State Park, the Erie Canal, near Lake Ontario, Lockport, and, yes, even in my own backyard. However, on two occasions, I rented a cabin at Letourneau Christian Camp in Canandaigua, NY for a few days to gain additional ideas. As I traveled home from my first visit, I had yet to determine a title for the book. My desire was that it would contain the word "creation", but how to work it into a title evaded me. As I drove and spoke to the Lord about this, low and behold, there in front of me was a Ford Echo. Suddenly, I got it: *Echoes of Creation*. The devotionals are echoes of love, hope, peace, and every other blessing, from the Father of creation.

My sincere hope is that the reader will grow closer in their relationship with Jesus by reading and thinking on these devotionals. Perhaps you will meet Jesus for the very first time, but wherever you are on your spiritual journey, it is my prayer that *Echoes of Creation* will take you one step further.

Hidden Treasure

"Fix these words of mine in your hearts and minds; tie them
as symbols on your hands and bind them on your foreheads.
Teach them to your children, talking about them when you
sit at home and when you walk along the road, when you lie
down and when you get up." (Deuteronomy 11:18-19)

Early one spring morning as I sat outside with my coffee, a squirrel
was digging up the ground with such vigor I figured he had to be
searching for food that had perhaps been stowed away the previous
autumn. I watched as he darted from one spot to another, retrieving
what was hidden in the ground after several minutes of digging,
and then running back to a hole in the nearby tree. I marveled
at how diligent he was in finding and sharing his treasure.

So, too, we as followers of Christ ought to be diligent in retrieving
and storing away heavenly treasures. God's word has an abundance
of treasure useful for, "teaching, rebuking, correcting, and training
in righteousness" (2 Timothy 3:16). When Christ-followers hide
God's word away in their hearts, they equip themselves to resist sin,
make godly decisions, and give their children a solid foundation
on which to build their faith and lives. In Matthew, we are warned
about storing up earthly treasures, such as public approval, monetary
gain, power, and material goods. These treasures turn our hearts
away from God and have no eternal benefit for those who are still in
need of Christ or us. We, as Christ-followers, ought to be found as
diligent as the squirrel in storing up God's treasure for heavenly use.

No Trespassing

"So flee youthful passions, and pursue righteousness,
faith, love and peace, along with those who call on the
Lord from a pure heart." (2 Timothy 2:22, ESV)

You can drive along rural roads or meander past a construction site, yet certain areas are off limits to outsiders, such as wooded pieces of property kept pristine for wild inhabitants or machines and materials that would be dangerous if tampered with by the wrong person. Whatever the reason, "No Trespassing" signs are present to keep certain people out, protecting them from impending harm.

In the Bible, God gives us "No Trespassing" signs too. Check out the book of Exodus with its Ten Commandments, where God bids us to refrain from adultery, stealing, envy, and idolatry. Paul, in the book of Ephesians, advises us to avoid foolish living, as is seen in sexual immorality, greed, or idle chatter/talk. Even Jesus Himself instructed us to be cautious of anger, lust, worry, and retaliation. To engage in such attitudes or behaviors is harmful to our witness for the Lord and inhibits the spread of the gospel in a world darkened with sin.

Rather, we are to clothe ourselves with the fruit of the Spirit, which is "...love, joy, peace, patience, kindness, goodness, faithfulness, gentleness, and self-control" (Galatians 6:22), so we can sow life, not destruction. By doing so, followers of Christ demonstrate that even though there are "No Trespassing" signs put up by God, heeding them results in a life that is more abundant, liberating, and productive.

Take Flight

"Therefore, there is now no condemnation for those who are in Christ Jesus, because through Christ Jesus the law of the Spirit of life set me free from the law of sin and death." (Romans 8:1-2)

In the elementary school where I work, the kindergarteners do a butterfly project every spring. The teachers allow the children to watch caterpillars eat leaves, form a cocoon, and then emerge as butterflies. The teachers then take the children outside to assist in releasing the butterflies from captivity.

In much the same way, we can be freed from the captivity, or bondage, of our sin. God sent His only Son, Jesus, to Earth as a sacrifice for the sins of the world. Jesus lived a perfect life here on Earth, facing the same temptations, trials, and conflicts we deal with in our lives, yet He remained free from sin. That's why He was the chosen sacrificial lamb. When we trust in what God did for us through Jesus' life, death, and resurrection, in that alone, we, too, can be released from captivity as a butterfly, to journey with God in a life filled with meaning and purpose.

Bugs!

"Therefore, O house of Israel, I will judge you, each one according to his ways, declares the Sovereign LORD. Repent! Turn away from all your offenses; then sin will not be your downfall. Rid yourselves of all the offenses you have committed, and get a new heart and a new spirit…For I take no pleasure in the death of anyone, declares the Sovereign LORD. Repent and live!" (Ezekiel 18:30-32)

Springtime and summer are noteworthy seasons for finding bugs indoors. It doesn't matter how careful one is about keeping windows and doors shut; they still seem to find a way in. Inevitably, you find yourself, just as I did one day, chasing bugs around the house in an attempt to be rid of them. Finally, I had one cornered in a kitchen window. Four swats later, he was definitely a goner. Four swats!

That got me to thinking: how many times does God have to hit us over the head before we give up a sinful habit or behavior or, even worse, initiate a positive one? Do we repent and rid ourselves of anger, lying, idolatry, or disobedience when God first reveals it to us? Sin in the life of a believer does not go undisciplined; just look at the Israelites' cycle of sin in the book of Judges. They repeatedly gave in to the sinful ways of their Canaanite neighbors, bringing God's wrath upon themselves time and again, only to become repentant and sin once more after God delivered them.

God calls us to true, heartfelt repentance. It is His desire that we continue to develop a Christ-like character, one that sets an example for others to follow. In Romans 6, Paul instructs us as followers of Christ to let go of our sinful ways now that we belong to Christ, that Jesus, not sin, should be our master. In doing so, we reflect the grace of God that forgives us our sin and leads others to do the same.

Authenticity

"But he said to me, 'My grace is sufficient for you, for my power is made perfect in weakness.' Therefore, I will boast all the more gladly of my weaknesses, so that the power of Christ may rest upon me. For the sake of Christ, then, I am content with weaknesses, insults, hardships, persecutions, and calamities. For when I am weak, then I am strong." (2 Corinthians 12:9-10 ESV)

Often I see trees that have been stripped of their bark, perhaps due to disease, weathering, or age. The trees have been exposed to outside elements more so than they were beforehand, making them vulnerable to further attack by animals, weather, and disease, sometimes to the point of death. This is symbolic of what can take place when those who follow Christ choose to become authentic in their relationships with other believers. We open ourselves up to attack by way of judgment, sometimes ridicule, rejection, and/or embarrassment by exposing those parts of ourselves that have lain dormant for so long. We may fear being used or taken advantage of by those with whom we become real. Often, this fear prevents others from hearing how the Lord has changed us and thus hinders positive change to take place in others. It is in becoming real, exposed, to others that we also reveal the might and power of a redeeming God. When the lost and discouraged see how God has moved in your life, they are able to recognize His ability to move in their lives, too.

Release

"Come to me, all you who are weary and burdened, and I will give you rest. Take my yoke upon you and learn from me, for I am gentle and humble in heart, and you will find rest for your souls. For my yoke is easy and my burden is light." (Matthew 11:28-30)

As I drove home from work one day, I spied a large bird, quite possibly an egret or heron, flying with a large object in its beak. It was obvious by the bird's struggle that the object's composition and size was too much of a burden, yet the bird continued to grasp the object as it flew onward.

How often do we catch ourselves holding onto things that are too cumbersome for us to handle? Past mistakes, current concerns, and future worries weigh us down, making the task of staying aloft very difficult. Jesus instructs us to take his burden, which is light, in exchange for giving our burdens over to Him. Only in this way can we soar above the difficulties of this life and demonstrate to others what a worthy Savior we have---one who desires to take our burdens, as He did at Calvary, and make them His own.

Hope

"Have I not commanded you? Be strong and courageous. Do not be terrified; do not be discouraged, for the LORD your God will be with you wherever you go." (Joshua 1:9)

Walking through the halls at work one day, I paused to pray at a large window. The sky was gray and cloudy with very little sunshine appearing. But as I stood there, gaps started developing in the clouds, forming smiley-face openings. Sunlight found its way and proceeded to stream through the openings. It reminded me of how, no matter where we are or what we're doing, God is always there someplace, shining through to offer us comfort and hope. This hope and comfort may come in the form of an encouraging word, an act of kindness, a timely message from God's word, or answered prayer. Whatever God chooses, though, it is our choice to accept His small blessing and move forward with the confidence that He has not abandoned us in those "gray" times.

Perspective

"Why are you downcast, O my soul? Why so disturbed within me? Put your hope in God, for I will yet praise him, my Savior and my God." (Psalm 42:5-6)

In the first week of May 2011, we enjoyed a four day stretch of sunshine, the most sunshine we'd had in Western New York since the beginning of September 2010, so the meteorologist claimed. One week later, we were back to the gray, dreary, rainy weather for several days. Once again I found myself starting to complain about the weather as I drove home from work one day, when the Lord opened my eyes to the green of trees budding, fields blooming, and bushes sprouting. Were it not for the rain, trees, fields, and bushes would not have abundant new life.

So it is in the lives of those who follow after Christ. We enjoy the "sunny" days where there are no conflicts or trials, when all is good. But when God chooses to throw in a little "rain", like conflicts with coworkers or family members, sleepless nights, illness, or financial struggles, we're all too ready to give up. It reminds me of when God delivered the Israelites from hostility, hard labor, and slavery in Egypt to enter the Promised Land. They complained about the kind of food they had to eat, rather than being thankful they had something to eat. When confronted with the Red Sea dilemma, they wanted to return to the life of slavery they had sought freedom from for so long. It's like the saying, "Look for the silver lining"; if we seek God's perspective we will see the blessing in the midst of it all.

Protection

"Train up a child in the way he should go; even when he is old, he will not depart from it." (Proverbs 22:6 ESV)

Canadian geese will sometimes build their nests alongside but also in the water. The parents sit on top of the nest to protect the young, incubating goslings. Some nests are built up into a mound, with the eggs nestled inside, safe from the elements and predators. Once hatched, the parents continue protecting their young by keeping them close together. As the young mature, they become aware of instinctive behaviors that will enable them to remain safe.

Human parents have fears with regards to their offspring. These could include abduction, chronic or terminal illness, addiction, bullying, and sexuality to name a few. God has provided parents with tools and wisdom to guide, protect, and nurture their young as well. Exposing our children to God's word early in life provides them with a standard for remaining safe and offering protection from many of life's dangers. Yet it is also a parent's responsibility to instruct their children in the ways of God so as they mature and leave the safety of their parent's "nest" to pursue a life of their own, they are able to discern right from wrong and know to whom they can turn when this earthly life does not give the answers they seek. Providing our children with a heritage of faith is by far the best protection we, as parents, can cultivate in them.

Transformation

"Do not conform any longer to the pattern of this world,
but be transformed by the renewing of your mind. Then
you will be able to test and approve what God's will is---
his good, pleasing and perfect will." (Romans 12:2)

There's a creek in a nearby park with a spillway that local fowl
visit frequently. I've observed ducks sitting at the spillway's
edge, precariously perched there until they float over the edge
and into the pool of water below. At times, they will be plunged
into the depths, although quickly bob back up to the surface.

How much this reminds me of ourselves as Christ-followers! Placing
ourselves in dangerous situations allows temptation to toy with our
mind and beliefs, which may eventually lead us into sin. We are
thinking precariously in presuming that we are strong enough to
resist and thus, forget our humanity, setting ourselves up for disaster.
It may be helpful to also consider the impact yielding to negative
temptations would have in our witness to others. Paul made mention
of this in Colossians when he instructed them to "…make the most
of every opportunity" (Colossians 4:5). Viewing every encounter as
an opportunity to be a witness for Christ, whether sharing the gospel
in word or action, can be one way we avoid yielding to temptation.

Be Still

"Even youths grow tired and weary, and young men stumble and fall; but those who hope in the LORD will renew their strength. They will soar on wings like eagles; they will run and not grow weary, they will walk and not be faint." (Isaiah 40:30-31)

Ever watch a duck trying to take flight from the surface of a lake or pond? Ducks don't have the same capability for flight that other birds do. They can only fly short distances before landing safely again. Their attempts to take flight are even more difficult than most other birds, as they often drop back down to the water several times before flying any great distance. It's almost as if they are striving in their own strength to perform a task. Sound familiar?

I know I have been guilty many a time for attempting to do something in my own strength, impatient to wait on God's timing. Yet as humans we are often in such a hurry to get something done we tend to ignore God's direction or His leading. If we would only learn to follow Him initially we would likely save ourselves time and effort. The benefits of doing so would be more eternal and beneficial in the long run. Waiting on God is never a poor choice; it is in the waiting that God often reveals Himself and builds our ability to trust Him more than ever.

Light

"You are the light of the world. A city on a hill cannot be hidden. Neither do people light a lamp and put it under a bowl. Instead, they put it on its stand, and it gives light to everyone in the house. In the same way, let your light shine before men, that they may see your good deeds and praise your Father in heaven." (Matthew 5:14-16)

I think it most beautiful when the sun is "caught" behind billowing clouds, its brightness unseen, except for the glistening edges of the clouds. The light is hidden from those who hunger for its warmth and brightness, who are waiting anxiously for their hope of sunshine to materialize.

I have often thought about this image and what it reveals about the light of Jesus. As followers of Christ, we have immediate access to God's presence through the Bible, prayer, and fellowship with other believers. In addition, we are commanded by Jesus Himself to take the Light of His word into the world to dispel darkness and give hope to those walking in sin. In doing so, we are spreading the warmth of God's eternal love, hope, and peace to others, rather than allowing the light of our faith to sit upon a shelf at home.

Clouds

"Find rest, O my soul, in God alone; my hope comes
from him. He alone is my rock and my salvation; he is
my fortress, I will not be shaken." (Psalm 62:5-6)

Have you ever wondered about clouds? Oh, we all know they
consist of tiny water droplets that evaporate from oceans, rivers,
puddles, lakes, and such. The water condenses mid-air and collects
into large masses to produce clouds. But have you ever wondered
how they float along with the breeze full of rain, sleet, snow, or
hail and never sink to the ground? How can it be that water in
our bodies causes such intense weight gain yet clouds remain
suspended in the sky as if held there by some invisible force?

In the same sense, God's presence is an invisible force that holds us
up when the burdens of this life weigh us down. Scripture tells us
time and again of how His abiding Spirit is "an ever present help in
trouble" (Psalm 46:1). Other passages go on to say, "I will uphold you
with my righteous right hand" (Isaiah 41:10); "…the Lord your God
goes with you; he will never leave you nor forsake you" (Deuteronomy
31:6). No matter what we face, we have a God who wants to be our
help in times of trouble! Look to Him, the author and finisher of your
faith, the one and only, true, omnipresent God, to bear you up.

Fences

"When all our enemies heard about this, all the surrounding nations were afraid and lost their self-confidence, because they realized that this work had been done with the help of our God." (Nehemiah 6:16)

I was observing my son and daughter-in-law as they put fencing up in their front yard, eagerly digging holes, placing posts, and attaching sections of fence to one another. As they worked, they discovered several pieces of wood that had obvious flaws in them, visible to the naked eye, that may have prevented them from being usable as part of the fence. My son was quite annoyed by this and stated, "I'll have to take these back and exchange them for better ones." My daughter-in-law replied, "They're still good; just put them on the other side where they won't be seen."

Isn't this an awesome picture of how God uses us despite our imperfections? Look at Moses when God called on him to deliver the Israelites out of Egypt. Moses gave the excuse that he couldn't speak well, but God used him anyway. David's youth and smallness didn't prevent God from using him to slay the giant Goliath. Paul revealed that he struggled with a "thorn in my flesh" (2nd Cor. 12:7,) yet his testimonies encourage churches even today. So don't think your physical, mental, or emotional weaknesses cannot be used by God. God's power and strength are displayed when we commit our weaknesses and imperfections to Him.

Weathered by Life

"Consider it pure joy, my brothers, whenever you face trials of many kinds, because you know that the testing of your faith develops perseverance. Perseverance must finish its work so that you may be mature and complete, not lacking anything." (James 1:2-4)

On my way to visit a friend, I stopped by the Niagara River for a spell. As I stooped near the water's edge, a piece of driftwood caught my eye. I reached in and pulled it out. Although the bark had been removed by the water's action, five unevenly distributed knots remained along the wood's length.

I pondered how one's life could be represented by that piece of wood. If the length of the wood was your timeline, the absence of its bark and the presence of knots could represent different trials you endured that God eventually used for His glory and honor. The loss of a loved one, marital difficulties, rebellious children, and illness are just a few. At times, trials may occur so close together, making them more difficult to bear and harder to see what God's purpose could be. However, God is always faithful, even though we may choose to ignore Him in our pain and anguish. In the end, He is glorified when we encourage others that are facing similar difficulties. Romans 8:28 states that "in all things God works for the good of those who love him". He uses the trials of our lives to mold us, make us more Christ-like, and expand our opportunities to serve Him.

Unity in the Body

"I in them and you in me. May they be brought to complete
unity to let the world know that you sent me and have
loved them even as you have loved me." (John 17:23)

Water falls upon the earth and collects in oceans, ponds, lakes,
rivers, streams, and creeks. Over time each drop will participate
in a continuous cycle that replenishes the earth with an endless
water supply. Its repetitive mission is to evaporate, condensate, and
precipitate. Were it not for water's united action the earth would be a
vast desert land, lacking essential life-giving support water provides.
Without it, life would vanish from the face of our lush planet.

Just as the unity of many droplets of water are vital in supporting
life on earth, the unity of believers is critical to the life of a church.
King David wrote that unity is "pleasant" and "precious" (Psalm
133:1, 2), that the Lord "bestows his blessing, even life forevermore"
(Psalm 133:3b) upon those who work towards unity in the church.
Unfortunately, many churches have suffered greatly with regards
to unity when disagreements occurred between believers. Be a
follower of Jesus who strives to maintain unity amongst believers
and a positive force in restoring unity when it comes under attack by
committing yourself to prayer and working together in humility.

Accountability

"My brothers, if one of you should wander from the truth and someone should bring him back, remember this: Whoever turns a sinner from the error of his way will save him from death and cover over a multitude of sins." (James 5:19-20)

Seeing two ducks in a pond beside one another creates an image of accountability and encouragement in my mind. Whenever one went under to grab a bite, the other rested upon the water's surface, patiently waiting for the other to emerge. Once it does, the other submerges to get his meal. They never seem to be far apart from one another, but when they are, it doesn't take long for them to pair back up again.

Our walk with Jesus is much the same. We benefit from having close relationships with other Christ-followers to provide the encouragement we need when struggling with sin or trials. When we "go under" from the weight of sin, burdens, or distractions, we sometimes fall into the mindset that Jesus has abandoned us. Yet we have the opportunity to walk alongside another believer to help us during those times. When the New Testament disciples faced difficulties, they encouraged one another and held each another accountable. Paul initiated, developed, and maintained relationships with Timothy, Barnabus, and others to assist him. Who holds you accountable?

Mushrooms

"This is the message we have heard from him and proclaim to you, that God is light, and in him is no darkness at all. If we say we have fellowship with him while we walk in darkness, we lie and do not practice the truth. But if we walk in the light, as he is in the light, we have fellowship with one another, and the blood of Jesus his Son cleanses us from all sin." (1st John 1:5-7, ESV)

I spied a towering tree with huge mushrooms attached to the trunk as I hiked through a forest. Now if I understand correctly, mushrooms are a type of fungi, a plant that grows in dark, damp places. So why were they growing up the side of a tree trunk towards the sunlight? Fascinating, I thought, that something so used to thriving in darkness would actually strive for the light. Was it aware that some difficulties could occur in such an environment?

How much like those mushrooms followers of Christ should be, reaching for the light to escape sin's decay and darkness! Jesus states in John 8:12, "I am the light of the world. Whoever follows me will never walk in darkness, but will have the light of life." If you have trusted in Jesus as your Lord and Savior you should no longer be living in the darkness of sin, even though we live in a sinful world.

Wounded

"For I was hungry and you gave me something to eat, I was thirsty and you gave me something to drink, I was a stranger and you invited me in, I needed clothes and you clothed me, I was sick and you looked after me, I was in prison and you came to visit me." (Matthew 25:35-36)

Many a carcass can be seen lying along our roadways no matter what the season. Springtime comes, accompanied by the arrival of heightened animal activity. Although nature lovers receive considerable joy in sighting deer, foxes, and rabbits, the sight of road kill torments us. Yet many of the wounded remain unattended, whether they need healing or a decent burial.

Do you know someone who is wounded? Is there a coworker, neighbor, relative, or perhaps a random stranger who could benefit from your tender mercies and care? Remember the man beaten, robbed, and left for dead in the parable of the Good Samaritan? Two men had already walked by this poor soul without even casting a glance his way. Yet the Samaritan not only approached the victim, he cared for him by dressing his wounds and providing for further care. There are many people today in need of physical, emotional, spiritual, and mental care. Many who are often too proud to ask for help, yet if offered they would gladly receive it. Those who seek to care for the less fortunate by using the strengths and gifts God has given you have a heavenly inheritance waiting for them.

Effective Image

"All Scripture is breathed out by God and profitable for teaching, for reproof, for correction, and for training in righteousness, that the man of God may be competent, equipped for every good work." (2nd Timothy 3:16-17, ESV)

Observing a duck as it preened itself stirred curiosity in me. The meticulous duck nudged, flapped, and pecked at its wings for several minutes. I had heard that birds preen their feathers for the purpose of bringing essential oils to the surface. Afterward, I discovered it also serves to align the feathers for more aerodynamic flight; makes feathers more attractive to a mate; encourages bonding between mates during courtship rituals; and removes parasites from the feathers. In one sense preening could be considered an act of pride yet it also serves to make birds more effective in other areas as well.

What better way to grow as a believer than to engage in biblical "preening" each day. Those with a strong desire to know and understand God's promises, recognize and repent of sin, find a Christian spouse, and establish unity among ministry workers know what steps to take for these things to be fulfilled. By committing scripture to memory, spending time studying God's word, and engaging in prayer consistently, one can be certain to accomplish such goals. Psalm 37:4 states, "Delight yourself in the LORD and he will give you the desires of your heart." Engaging in Christ-like behaviors such as these will not only glorify God, but develop a rich legacy for those you leave behind and bring forth a multitude of blessings from God's hand.

Ripple Effect

"Do not be deceived: God cannot be mocked. A man reaps what
he sows. The one who sows to please his sinful nature, from
that nature will reap destruction; the one who sows to please the
Spirit, from the Spirit will reap eternal life." (Galatians 6:7-8)

Skipping rocks across the water's surface is one of my grandkids'
favorite pastimes during the summer. If they're lucky, a rock can skip
up to eight times before sinking to the bottom. Other times the rock
plops into the water without any skipping at all. Ever notice the ripple
effect, how it closely resembles the point at which an earthquake
strikes and reverberates? The ripples seem to go on and on before
stopping completely, moving the seen and unseen in their path.

Sin and obedience can be like that, often without us ever taking notice
of it. We tell a lie, cheat, commit adultery, or share gossip, never
realizing how our sin may be negatively impacting others. This is a
recurring theme in the lives of believers. When Joshua led the Israelites
to defeat Jericho, the sin of Achan resulted in his death and the loss
of his family and possessions. Simultaneously, this ripple effect can
be true of our obedience. When we choose to obey God's word and
His calling on our lives, blessings abound. Paul and Silas, in Acts
16, were obedient in singing praises to God while in prison. This act
resulted in their release from prison, and the jailer and his family's
salvation. Inevitably, our obedience will take us much further for the
Kingdom than our sin and enable us to bring many more along!

Open Palms

"So the Twelve gathered all the disciples together and said, 'It would not be right for us to neglect the ministry of the word of God in order to wait on tables. Brothers, choose seven men from among you who are known to be full of the Spirit and wisdom. We will turn this responsibility over to them and give our attention to prayer and the ministry of the word." (Acts 6:2-4)

Palm trees are quite different in their appearance. The trunks extend upward to great heights, and culminate in a spread of frond-like branches at the top, resembling those of ferns. If you look closely at the trunk of a palm tree, though, you'll notice that it's nothing like a typical tree. It appears to consist of overlapping sections in layers all the way up the trunk. Most trees have trunks that are solid, with no apparent support until you chop part of it away and see the rings inside. I imagine a palm tree's structure provides it with a certain measure of strength.

The church is in need of strength that comes in layers as well. The main component is Jesus Himself, the cornerstone of the church (1st Peter 2). A church that is established on the sure foundation of Jesus needs a leader, typically in the form of a pastor. The pastor needs solid, unified support to come around him in order to do the work of making and shepherding disciples successfully. We, as believers and followers of Jesus Christ, are called upon to offer these leaders support in the way of prayer, tithes, service, and encouragement so the work of the church moves forward.

Seasons of Grace

"But his delight is in the law of the LORD, and on his law he
meditates day and night. He is like a tree planted by streams
of water that yields fruit in its season, and its leaf does not
wither. In all that he does, he prospers." (Psalm 1:2-3, ESV)

No matter what the season, trees array their splendor. But one of the
most striking winter sights for me are tree boughs laden with snow. It
doesn't matter how large or small the limbs of a tree may be, snow will
rest on its branches just the same. Snow blankets a tree's nakedness
with a covering so pure and white that it may be easy to forget how
lush and colorful they are any other time of year. Despite the natural
trials trees face each season, they continue to be a portrait of beauty.

Each of our lives has its share of victories and failures as we
journey along, too. We celebrate joyous milestones like births,
graduations, marriages, and retirements. No matter how
big or small the accomplishment, we delight in celebrating
it. Consider the Israelites when they reached the Promised
Land, Ruth's marriage to Boaz, and Jesus' birth. Each of
these situations produced joyful songs of praise to God.

On the other hand, we also face seasons of doubt and failure, as
in divorce, bankruptcy, or losing our job. These we can barely get
through, let alone find reason to glorify God. The Israelites doubted
God's provision when they left Egypt. Samson failed when he shared
the secret of his strength with Delilah. Job faced doubts when God
allowed Satan to take away all his family and possessions. Yet the
Lord deemed them worthy to undergo these trials, and then to rise
above afterward. When we choose to rely on God in all seasons
of life, He is willing and able to see us through victoriously.

Under Attack

"For though we live in the world, we do not wage war as
the world does. The weapons we fight with are not the
weapons of the world. On the contrary, they have divine
power to demolish strongholds." (2nd Corinthians 10:3-4)

Three small birds may seem totally harmless to a casual spectator
who just happens to glance upwards. But one day I paused long
enough to notice that these small birds were bombarding a large
turkey buzzard mid-air. I suspected the turkey buzzard had made
an attempt at stealing eggs or young from his attackers' nests,
bringing their wrath upon himself. Although I felt a slight twinge
of sympathy for the buzzard, I knew that if it had been my young
under attack, I would have fought back fiercely as well.

As followers of Jesus, we are frequently under attack. The enemy
"prowls around like a roaring lion looking for someone to devour"
(1st Peter 5:8), taking every opportunity to lead us astray through
deception. The enemy knows how, when, and where to strike,
often catching us off guard. He fills our minds with lies, doubts,
and fears about our redemption. He leads us to believe that we
are unworthy of Christ's love and forgiveness. In order to resist
him, we need to "put on the full armor of God" (Eph. 6:11). Equip
yourself with the truth of God's word so you can "extinguish all the
flaming arrows of the evil one" (Eph. 6:16). Reading, memorizing,
and applying God's word strengthens us for the enemy's attacks.

Oasis

"The LORD is my rock, my fortress, and my deliverer; my
God is my rock in whom I take refuge. He is my shield and
the horn of my salvation, my stronghold." (Psalm 18:2)

A stand of trees in an open field. A pool of water in the vast
dryness of a desert. An island in the midst of an ocean. All
of these could be considered an oasis, a refuge from physical,
emotional, or mental difficulties. We can expect to encounter
many such difficulties in the course of a lifetime. Looking for
an oasis during such times is a survival technique that may be
somewhat instinctive, yet we too often turn to worldly things to
provide long-term solace, peace, or wisdom. We attempt to escape
the pressures of life by enjoying a spa treatment, gym workout, or
vacation to find some relief, even though it may be short-lived.

Jesus has said, "Come to me, all you who are weary and burdened,
and I will give you rest. Take my yoke upon you and learn from me,
for I am gentle and humble in heart, and you will find rest for your
souls. For my yoke is easy and my burden is light" (Matthew 11:28-
30). Jesus is an oasis for this life! In Him, we find all that we need, no
matter what the need is. Turn your heart towards Him and find rest in
the midst of trials, peace in chaos, comfort in sadness, and wisdom in
confusion. His rich supply never empties and His care never ceases.

Beware!

"And even if our gospel is veiled, it is veiled to those who are perishing. The god of this age has blinded the minds of unbelievers, so that they cannot see the light of the gospel of the glory of Christ, who is the image of God." (2 Corinthians 4:3-4)

My early morning walks through meadows or along shorelines could be shrouded in fog, especially during summer and autumn months. It acts as a veil that prevents me from having a clear view of my surroundings. If I have my mind and heart focused on other things as I walk, these distract me from remaining aware of any dangers. When the warmth and brightness of sunlight finally cause the fog to dissipate, the truth of my surroundings appear.

The enemy blinds the spiritual eyes of unbelievers in the same fashion. His deceptions of worldly gain, such as wealth, fame, and power, cause unbelievers to think they are obtaining eternity. Though the gospel has been shared with them, the enemy's deceptions prevent them from accepting it. Until the Spirit of truth removes the veil of doubt, deceit, and uncertainty, and the Son's truth shines through, they will go on living in darkness.

Comfortable

"In fact, though by this time you ought to be teachers, you
need someone to teach you the elementary truths of God's
word all over again. You need milk, not solid food! Anyone
who lives on milk, being still an infant, is not acquainted with
the teaching about righteousness." (Hebrews 5:12-13)

On one occasion I happened to be perched on a fallen log near a
lake when I spied a blue heron a few feet away. He was standing
at the lake's edge ever so quietly, basking in the sunlight,
content to stay put for what seemed like an eternity to me. He
occasionally gazed into the water, possibly searching for a bite
to eat, and I began to wonder why he didn't fly off to look for
food in another spot. I guess he was comfortable staying put.

As believers we often get comfortable with regards to our spiritual
maturity. For many of us, complacency is a way to avoid pain,
conflict, and change. Yet spiritual maturity is obtained by applying
the truth of God's word to our lives and experiencing suffering or
trials. The death of a loved one, job changes, a sudden move, or
chronic illness are all circumstances that God allows to mature His
followers by drawing us close to Him and into His word. We are
easily deceived when we choose to be listeners of the word rather
than doers (James 1). Allowing the truth of God's word to take root
in us equips us for ministering to others, defeating the enemy, and
deepening our personal relationship with Jesus. As we mature, we need
to continue seeking the "solid food" (Hebrews 5:14) He has for us.

Abundant Life

"If anyone would come after me, he must deny himself and take up his cross daily and follow me. For whoever wants to save his life will lose it, but whoever loses his life for me will save it. What good is it for a man to gain the whole world, and yet lose or forfeit his very self?" (Luke 9:23-25)

Once while walking through a historical cemetery, I happened upon a young deer strolling just a few feet away from me. As peculiar as it seemed initially, I thought, "Why not? A cemetery is a quiet, secluded place with few people so I suppose it's possible to see a deer wandering about." The familiar chorus, "As a deer panteth for the water, so my soul longeth after Thee," stirred in my head and I began to sing the tune softly. How amazing that here, in the midst of death, I discovered life!

How much like that is our walk with Jesus? As we grow in our relationship with Him, we need to consistently evaluate how best to use our time, money, strengths, and experiences for the Kingdom of God. What plans do you have for your life? What skills or strengths do you have that can be used to help others grow in their faith? Early Christians allowed their possessions and jobs to be purposeful for God. Seek to please God with all you are and have. Your life will be an abundant, joy-filled journey.

Obstacles

"Therefore, since we are surrounded by such a great cloud
of witnesses, let us throw off everything that hinders and the
sin that so easily entangles, and let us run with perseverance
the race marked out for us. Let us fix our eyes on Jesus…
who endured such opposition from sinful men, so that you
will not grow weary and lose heart." (Hebrews 12:1, 2a, 3)

Walking through a state forest, one would expect to see many
plants flourishing along creek beds, around the bases of trees, in
open meadows, and on the forest floor. But on this particular day I
happened upon a lush, green plant in a most peculiar spot: between
two large boulders, far away from any soil or water supply, in
an entirely shaded area. I thought it interesting that a plant could
grow in such a spot at all, let alone flourish so beautifully.

Remind you of anything? How about Daniel, when he, along with
many other Israelites, was taken into captivity by the Babylonians?
Although Daniel was in a foreign land, God used his lion's den
experience to reveal His power to King Darius. The paralytic's friends
broke through the barriers of crowds and culture to bring their friend
to Jesus and be healed. And let's not forget Joseph, whose captivity in
the hands of the Egyptians led to the provision of food for thousands
during a lengthy famine. The woman who dared to fight crowds so
she could touch the hem of Jesus' garment, trusting she would be
healed, showed immense faith. These people looked beyond their
obstacles to see opportunities for healing, growth, and salvation. We
can grow anywhere God takes us when we place our faith in Jesus.

Passion

"For Christ's love compels us, because we are convinced that one died for all, and therefore all died. And he died for all, that those who live should no longer live for themselves but for him who died for them and was raised again." (2 Corinthians 5:14-15)

The mere thought of campfires and bonfires elates my spirit, promising goodness from the songs sung around them to the savoring of roasted hotdogs and s'mores. A great fire needs fuel, typically in the form of wood, whether it's lumber, logs, or twigs. Once the fuel source stops, though, the fire dies down to glowing red-orange embers, smoldering ashes, and decaying wood. The passion and energy of the fire is lost. More fuel must be added to bring the fire back to life.

So it is with the passion of living for Jesus. Believers need fellowship, prayer, and God's word to fuel their passion. In Revelation 3, Jesus addresses the lukewarm church of Laodicea. The people of this church allowed wealth and position to extinguish their passion for the Lord. When we choose to neglect adding fuel to our faith, feeding the desires of our flesh instead, we, too, will fizzle out in our passion of living for Christ. Surrounding ourselves with believers, remaining steadfast in God's word, and serving others assist us in remaining passionate for Jesus. Are you passionate for the Lord?

Abiding

"Abide in me, and I in you. As the branch cannot bear fruit
by itself, unless it abides in the vine, neither can you, unless
you abide in me. I am the vine; you are the branches. Whoever
abides in me and I in him, he it is that bears much fruit, for
apart from me you can do nothing." (John 15:4-5, ESV)

My parents loved to grow strawberries in their home garden
so they could enjoy the benefits of strawberry shortcake and
homemade jam throughout the year. A bed of straw would cover
the plants each spring to prevent a surplus of weeds from choking
the strawberries out. The straw would remain through winter,
too, for additional protection from the cold and snow. I remember
one spring, as the plants began to grow, my mother discovering
that some of them were not bearing blossoms. As she dug beneath
the layer of straw, she found the reason: slugs had eaten away at
the stems and roots, cutting them off from their food supply.

Jesus calls His own to abide in Him so we can produce fruit for
the Kingdom in this life. Just as strawberry plants need to stay
connected to the stem and roots in order to produce fruit, so, too, we
must abide in and connect with Jesus to reach the lost, encourage
new believers, and develop an effective ministry. Paul, one of
Jesus' greatest followers, relied heavily upon Christ to be effective
in what he was called to do. In all of humanity, there is not one
who is capable of doing God's work on their own. We must abide
with Him so His plans can be accomplished in and through us.

Scripture Index

Symbols

1st John 1
  5-7, ESV 23
2 Corinthians 4
  3-4 32
2 Corinthians 5
  14-15 38
2 Corinthians 12
  9-10 ESV 6
2nd Corinthians 10
  3-4 30
2nd Timothy 3
  16-17, ESV 25
2 Timothy 2
  22, ESV 2

A

Acts 6
  2-4 27

D

Deuteronomy 11
  18-19 1

E

Ezekiel 18
  30-32 5

G

Galatians 6
  7-8 26

H

Hebrews 5
  12-13 34
Hebrews 12
  1, 2a, 3 36

I

Isaiah 40
  30-31 13

J

James 1
  2-4 19
James 5
  19-20 21
John 15
  4-5, ESV 40
John 17
  23 20
Joshua 1
  9 8

L

Luke 9
  23-25 35

M

Matthew 5
  14-16 15
Matthew 11
  28-30 7

Matthew 25
  35-36 24

N

Nehemiah 6
  16 17

P

Proverbs 22
  6 ESV 10
Psalm 1
  2-3, ESV 28
Psalm 18
  2 31
Psalm 42
  5-6 9
Psalm 62
  5-6 16

R

Romans 8
  1-2 3
Romans 12
  2 12